Thor "Bushman Ollie" Janson

Belize
Land of the Free by the Carib Sea

Contents

Belize: Many Roots, One People.

Twenty thousand years ago Central America was a very different place than we know today. A vast amount of water was trapped in the northern glaciers at the end of the last ice age and the Caribbean Sea was much lower than it is today. The land mass of Central America was much larger. The climate was cooler and the forests were made up of temperate pine species and inhabited by many animals no longer present today such as wild horses, giant ground sloths, and mastodons.

According to archaeologists the first wave of human colonists arrived in Belize some 12,000 years ago, the progeny of the pioneering Asian explorers who had crossed over the Bering Land Bridge around 20,000 BC and thereafter slowly migrated south to finally reach the Caribbean. Primitive Neolithic tools were uncovered at the Richmond Hill dig in Orange Walk District dating from approximately 9000 BC and are the earliest evidence of human activity in Belize. The first permanent settlements did not appear until several thousand years later with the advent of domesticated plant and animal species and above all the arrival of cultivated corn which provided the foundation for the emergence of Mayan Civilization.

Around 300 BC we begin to see rapid cultural advancement with the development of beautiful monumental architecture and large stratified population centers ruled over by an aristocratic priest class. The period spanning the years from 500 to 850 AD finds Mayan Civilization in full flower and many large cities, rivaling in sophistication and prosperity any in the world, were built. It is estimated that at their height the Maya of Belize numbered as many as 2,000,000 souls. Then, in a mysterious series of events still not well understood, Mayan Civilization went into decline and by 900 AD most of the cities had been abandoned and the untamed jungles and rain forests returned to dominate the landscape.

The next wave of human colonization began with the Spanish "discovery" of the Americas. In the early 1500's these European discoverers were greeted by as many as 200,000 Maya who resided in the land now called Belize. Later on British buccaneers chose the coast of Belize as one of their favorite hide outs as they preyed upon Spanish

Merchant ships provisioning the early colonies in Central America and transporting plunder back to the courts of the Old World. It is interesting to note that the word buccaneer comes from the Maya word "buccan" for dried manatee meat. This must have been an important staple for the British pirates. By the mid-seventeenth century some of the British decided to establish permanent settlements dedicated to the exploitation of logwood which was in great demand in Europe and was used as a dye for textiles. These early settlers became known as the Baymen and later on they established their capital on St. George's Caye. More laborers were required and people of African origin were brought in from Honduras and the West Indies to work in the logging camps. The melding of African and European elements gave rise to a new people: the Creole, who went on to create a unique Belizean culture all their own.

The land of Belize became part of the British empire as the colony of British Honduras in 1862 and the nineteenth century saw the arrival of many new colonists. "Hindu" laborers were brought over from India and settled mainly in the south. The Garinagu, a new culture created by the amalgamation of Nigerian and Amerindian people, began to arrive from Honduras and soon established villages in the area of Stann Creek. Mestizos, of mixed Spanish and Mayan blood, came over from Mexico and populated the north and west. Kek'chi Indians from the region of Alta Verapaz in Guatemala slowly began to colonize the jungles of the far south. More recently people from all over the world have landed in Belize to add to her unique cultural mix. These include people of North and Central American, Mid Eastern, Asian, West Indian, and European origin.

British Honduras attained independence from England on September 21, 1981 and became part of the British Commonwealth. Since then the new country has been going through all the growth pains and exhilaration of youth and adolescence. Agriculture, fisheries, and tourism have all been expanding and ecology has become the national passion. Belize is blessed with a unique cultural and natural diversity and all the elements necessary for a peaceful and prosperous future are abundantly present. This new Central American nation in the heart of the Caribbean is proving that a diverse cultural rainbow of people from around the planet can unite together for peace, strength and freedom.

Crooked Tree Cashew Festival

There is no better place in the country to get a feeling for the unique Belizean Creole culture than at the little village of Crooked Tree and one of the best times to visit is during the annual Cashew Festival which takes place during the month of May. The people here trace their roots back to the mingling of African and European tribal elements during the early colonization of Belize and Crooked Tree is one of the oldest inland settlements in the country. The village stands in the middle of a huge cashew grove and the festival takes place when the large trees are heavy with ripe fruit. Groovy vibes are provided by world famous Mr. Peter's Boom and Chime Bruckdown Band. Bruckdown is the real Belizean music which was born in the early logging camps when the rum flowed and the mood turned festive. Today there are only a few Bruckdown bands still playing and Mr. Peters Boom and Chime is considered a national treasure. During the festival there are many special events including the presentation of the Cashew Queen and here beautiful little Blossoms. The girls do their thing and entertain the crowd with special dances where traditional moves are combined with new styles. Other events include a bike race, craft exhibits, dances, and of course a massive barbecue where spicy chicken is served up with rice and beans and washed down with ice cold glasses of delicious cashew wine.

Crooked Tree is also home of the Crooked Tree Wildlife Sanctuary which preserves 3000 acres of prime estuarine habitat and includes four large lagoons along with swamps and waterways. Founded in 1984, the reserve provides critical habitat for migratory birds and during the winter months hosts large flocks of avian travelers. One of the reserve's most famous visitors is the giant Jabiru stork which is the largest flying bird in the New World and has a wing span of eight feet! Among the other creatures which may be seen at the reserve include iguanas, coatimundis, howler monkeys, crocodiles, turtles, jaguarundis, kinkajous, and dozens of butterfly species.

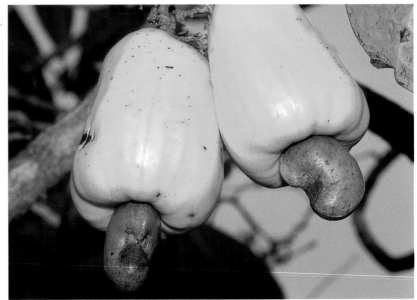

Crooked Tree Wildlife Sanctuary
[UPPER LEFT]

Crooked Tree Wildlife Sanctuary
[LOWER LEFT]

Burrell Boom River Regatta
[BELOW]
  Little Creole girl dressed in her Sunday best.

Burrell Boom River Regatta
[OPPOSITE UPPER LEFT]
  Chillin' in Boom Creek on a hot afternoon!

Burrell Boom River Regatta
[OPPOSITE UPPER RIGHT]
  We won! Winners of a traditional pit pan race are jubilant over their hard won victory.

Burrell Boom River Regatta
[OPPOSITE LOWER LEFT]
  The competition is fierce as competitors struggle to take the lead in the wheelbarrow race.

Passion Fruit Flower
[OPPOSITE LOWER RIGHT]

Rainforest Coffee at Gallon Jug Experimental Farm, Orange Walk District
[OPPOSITE UPPER LEFT AND RIGHT]

One of numerous "green" industries at Gallon Jug, the Rainforest Coffee Project produces world class 100% Arabica coffee while preserving the original rain forest. Only the understory of the forest is cleared to make room to plant the coffee while the rain forest diversity remains intact providing critical habitat for innumerable species including endangered migratory birds, many small mammals, and countless insect varieties which are crucial elements for the healthy functioning of the natural ecology.

World Famous Chan Chich Lodge
[OPPOSITE LOWER LEFT]

Located in the middle of a vast rain forest and surrounded by a Classic Period Maya site, Chan Chich receives visitors from around the world and provides a first class base from which to explore the pristine jungle.

Jaguar: The King of the Belizean Jungle
[OPPOSITE LOWER RIGHT]

Howler Monkey at the Bermudian Landing Community Baboon Sanctuary
[UPPER LEFT]

This unique reserve for the endangerd black howler money depends on the participation of over 100 local landowners who have agreed to protect the broadleaf forest on their land to provide a refuge for the "baboons."

Bermudian Landing Village
[UPPER RIGHT]

D's Cool Spot for an ice cold Belikin on a hot afternoon!

Morpho Butterfly
[LOWER LEFT]

The mystical "blue flash" of the Belizean rain forest.

Kinkajou
[LOWER RIGHT]

This medium-size rain forest omnivore spends its days searching the canopy for foods which include insects, eggs, fruits and small reptiles.

Oscillated Turkey
[UPPER LEFT]
These large birds are found in abundance in the Gallon Jug-Chan Chich Reserve area. They spend most of the day foraging on the forest floor but will fly up into the trees for safety when they feel threatened.

Tamandua (Ant Bear)
[UPPER RIGHT]
This medium-sized anteater spends its days searching the forest canopy for insects.

Tree Frog
[LOWER LEFT]
These superbly camouflaged tree dwellers are equipped with suction-cup finger pads that allow them to defy gravity.

Citreoline Trogon
[LOWER RIGHT]
These small relatives of the Resplendent Quetzal are common in the lowland rain forests of Belize. They have the uncommon habit of building their homes in active hornet nests but, for reasons as yet not well understood, the hornets do not bother the birds.

Wildflowers
[BELOW]

Butterfly
[OPPOSITE]

Corozal Town
[OPPOSITE UPPER LEFT]

The restored colonial market houses the Corozal Cultural Museum.

Orange Walk Town
[OPPOSITE UPPER RIGHT]

With a population of 20,000, Orange Walk is the largest town in the North.

Sugar Cane
[OPPOSITE LOWER LEFT]

Sugar is the lifeblood of the northern Economy. Trucks arrive at the refinery loaded with freshly cut cane which will be juiced and evaporated into sugar. The bi-product molasses is made into rum.

Belize Sugar Industry Trade Exhibit at the annual Trade Show
[OPPOSITE LOWER RIGHT]

Sugar cane produces many useful products: brown sugar, white sugar, molasses, rum, alcohols, and cattle feed.

Maya Ruins of Altun Ha
[RIGHT]

Located some 40 miles north of Belize City and five miles west of the sea, Altun Ha is one of the largest and most impressive ancient Mayan sites in Belize. The city was occupied for more than 1000 years until the collapse of the Classic Maya around 950 A.D. During its height Altun Ha was populated by more than 10,000 souls. At that time the land that we now call Belize is estimated to have been home to as many as two million Maya who inhabited many independent and powerful city-states.

Rum
[BELOW]

A wide variety of rum and cane liquor beverages are produced at the northern distilleries.

Keel-billed Toucan
[LEFT]

The keel-billed toucan is the National Bird of Belize, this toucan inhabits the lowland rain forest.

Butterfly, Shipstern Wildlife Reserve
[BELOW]

The Maya Ruins of Altun Ha
[OPPOSITE UPPER LEFT]

An important ceremonial and trade center during the Classic period.

The Maya Ruins of Laminai
[OPPOSITE UPPER RIGHT]

One of the most impressive Mayan sites in Belize, Laminai is located on the shore of the New River Lagoon and its original name "Lamanyan" means "submerged crocodile." The jungle atmosphere makes this one of the nicest sites in Belize. The city was continually occupied from 500 BC until the arrival of the Europeans. One of the most outstanding features at Laminai is the 50 foot high Late Preclassic temple called "El Castillo." When first built, around the year 100 BC, this was the largest structure in the entire Mayan world.

The Maya Ruins of Lamanai
[OPPOSITE LOWER LEFT AND RIGHT]

Detail of Classic Period ceramic artifacts found at the site.

Belize City

[OPPOSITE]

The largest city in Belize with a population of around 60,000, this is home to people of many ethnic groups although the Creole, descendents of Africans and Baymen, form the majority. Belize City has a unique atmosphere unlike anywhere else. Located right on the Caribbean shore, the city has been virtually destroyed two times by hurricanes. The last time was when Hurricane Hattie slammed into the coast with winds of up to 240 M.P.H. After that the government decided to rebuild the capitol 50 miles inland and founded Belmopan. But Belize City residents prefer the cool ocean breeze and few moved. Belize remains today a vibrant metropolis although in 1999 Hurricane Mitch nearly leveled the city again.

Belize City

[UPPER RIGHT]

Store fronts along Regent Street.

Belize City

[LOWER LEFT]

School girls cross the Haulover Creek foot bridge during a field trip.

Belize City

[LOWER RIGHT]

The sailboats of the fishing fleet are anchored in Haulover Creek near the swing bridge at the heart of the city in a scene little changed from a century ago.

Government House Museum
[UPPER LEFT]
 Built in 1814, this was the British Governor's residence when he visited the colony. Today Government House is the site of a museum containing displays concerning the colonial history of the country as well as hosting a variety of art exhibits showcasing regional artists.

Belize City
[LOWER LEFT]
 First class hotels and accommodations can be found in both the north and south sides of the city.

Belize City Swing Bridge
[LOWER RIGHT AND OPPOSITE]
 Built in Liverpool, England and installed at Haulover Creek in 1923, this is the only manually operated swing bridge left in the Americas. At 5:30 AM and 5:30 PM terrestrial traffic crossing Haulover Creek is halted as a crew of eight men, using long poles inserted into the central capstan, slowly crank the bridge open allowing large boats to pass. Some city planners wanted to replace the Swing Bridge with a more modern version. Fortunately the scheme was squelched and this historic landmark will continue to be the symbol of the heart of Belize City for years to come.

Saint John's Cathedral

[OPPOSITE]

Completed in 1820, this is the oldest Anglican cathedral in Central America and one of the oldest buildings in Belize City. Saint John's is located at the southern end of Albert Street. The bricks with which it was built were brought over from England. It was here, between the years of 1815 and 1845, that the Kings of Mosquito Coast were crowned when the British Protectorate extended to include the coasts of Honduras and Nicaragua. The Miskito Indians were not friendly with the Spanish colonial authorities and preferred to form alliances with Britain. Their rulers were crowned in British Honduras and their children were baptized at Saint John's Cathedral.

Saint John's Cathedral

[RIGHT]

Detail of stained-glass window

Christmas in Belize City

[BELOW]

We three kings of orient are... Christmas traditionally is the biggest holiday of the year in the Creole community. It is a time of family gatherings, Christmas pageants, plenty of good food and rum punch and, in many homes, the annual installation of new linoleum flooring in what has become a rather unique custom of Belize City residents who like to start the new year off in style.

Belize-Lebanese Restaurant
[OPPOSITE LEFT]
Owner and chef Jehad Dergham welcomes visitors to sample his Middle East cuisine.

Battlefield Park
[OPPOSITE UPPER RIGHT]
Located in the heart of the city, Central Park was renamed Battlefield to commemorate the fiery political meetings which took place here between those favoring independence and others preferring colonial rule. Independence was won in 1981.

Belize City Christmas
[OPPOSITE LOWER RIGHT]
Santa consults with kids on matters of great importance! A bike, or a doll or a boom box...?

Reggae by de River
[UPPER RIGHT]
A popular night spot located next to the Belcan Bridge which spans Haulover Creek.

Hindu Temple
[LOWER RIGHT]
Monica Narwani and Neetu Balani perform the Pooja Dance at Belize Hindu Temple.

Bruckdown Beat
[BELOW]
Master musician Mr. Lennox Blades is a legendary Bruckdown guitarist. Blades has also won fame in Belize as the inventor of everything from "Pink Glory" hair growing potion to specially designed animal traps.

"The Bitter! The Better!"
[OPPOSITE UPPER LEFT]
  Herb Day at the AGAPI Herb Center. Representatives display the famous FI DI MAN and FI DI WOMAN Belizean bitters: "powerful healing tonic that rejuvenates."

Barbecue!
[OPPOSITE UPPER RIGHT]
  Along with chicken, beef, and ribs, gibnut (a large rodent affectionately called "The Royal Rat" after Queen Elizabeth reportedly ate some during Her tour of the Colony and was said to have enjoyed it) and iguana are served.

School Girls attending Culture Day at the Baron Bliss Institute
[OPPOSITE LOWER LEFT]

Special event at Government House honoring senior citizens
[OPPOSITE LOWER RIGHT]

Cruising North Front Street
[UPPER RIGHT]

Culture Day at the Baron Bliss Institute
[LOWER LEFT]
  The marimba orchestra from San Jose Succotz performs Maya style Marimba music for Belize City youth at the annual Culture Day.

Culture Day at the Baron Bliss Institute
[LOWER RIGHT]
  Belizean Hula? Anything goes as traditional and innovative rhythms and dance moves are melded into a new, youthful synthesis.

Supreme Court Opening Ceremony
[OPPOSITE AND BELOW]

In January a special ceremony is organized for the official opening of the Supreme Court which is located in the heart of the city on Regent Street just south of Haulover Creek. The Supreme Court Judges review the Belize Defense Force Honor Guard.

At independence Belize decided to retain its place within the Commonwealth of Nations and its allegiance to the Queen of England, who is the official Head of State. The prime minister and the cabinet are chosen from the majority party in the lower house of the legislature and constitute the executive branch of government. Modeled along the Westminster-Whitehall form of government, the 28 member house of representatives is elected where as the eight member senate is appointed: five by the governor general on the advise of the prime minister, two by the opposition party and one by the Belize Advisory council. The prime minister and the appointed cabinet are all members of the National Assembly which makes the legislative branch a close reflection of the ruling party.

The Queen of the Bay
[RIGHT]

September is a busy month in Belize as we celebrate three major events: The commemoration of the Battle of St. Georges Caye, Independence Day and Carnival. This is an excellent time to visit the country for those interested in seeing Belize City at its very best. Each year The Queen of the Bay is elected to preside over the September Celebrations.

Independence Day Celebrations

Belize became an independent country on September 21, 1981 and since then every September has been a time of massive celebrations, parades, and special events. A special reenactment of the Battle of St. Georges Cay (opposite) was organized in 1998 to commemorate the 200th anniversary of the crucial battle with the Spanish which guaranteed the sovereignty of the British Colony. Member of the military band (upper left.) Independence day parade (upper middle and below.) A representative of the Wallace Clan (upper right) and a relative of one of the original Scottish settlers of Belize talks at the Independence Day ceremony. Some historians believe that the word Belize is a corruption of the name "wallace."

Belize City Carnival
[PAGES 32 THROUGH 39]

A tradition in Belize only since independence, the Carnival in September has grown year by year and now considered to be one of the largest and best organized in the entire Caribbean. Dance groups such as the Jump Street Posse and the Yarborough Youth vie for the honor of being judged the best. Preparation goes on all year long as every ounce of imagination and creativity go into the design and elaboration of the beautiful costumes. Each group selects one or several special carnival songs. Wild dance steps and choreographed march drills swing to the beat. Groups pass the reviewing stand at the National Stadium (opposite) during a last final fling in the evening of carnival.

Orange Walk Carnival, Orange Walk District

[Pages 40 and 41]

Not to be outdone by Belize City, Orange Walk has organized its own carnival sponsored, in part, by the northern sugar and rum industries. This carnival has a different flavor as the Mestizo Cultural element is strong in Orange Walk. Youths forming the parade groups begin many months in advance to prepare their hand made costumes and rehearse their carnival march steps.

" THE BEST IN THE WEST"

Heading west out from Belize City the road passes through an ever changing variety of habitats from mangrove forests and swamps, to pine-ridge savannah, and finally reaching the rolling hills of Cayo District. Cayo is somewhat cooler than the coast and the air is a bit dryer. Orange groves, cattle ranches, and corn fields create a peaceful pastoral scene. San Ignacio and Santa Elena are the largest towns followed by Benque Viejo del Carmen. The other settlements such as Bullet Tree Falls, Cala Creek, Cristo Rey, and Teakettle are quite small. Cayo is also home to the modern and prosperous Mennonite settlement of Spanish Lookout and to several "primitive" Mennonite settlements such as Barton Creek where the inhabitants have chosen to reject modern technology, such as radios, televisions, and automobiles, and live in quiet, tranquil peace.

Benque Viejo Del Carmen
[UPPER LEFT]
World famous HAWAII restaurant serves up ice cold beers and regional treats.

Christmas in Benque
[LOWER LEFT]

Branch Mouth Foot Bridge
[OPPOSITE]
Branch Mouth is located at the confluence of the Mopan and Macal Rivers. Local kids make their daily trek to school in San Ignacio.

Domino Championship
[UPPER LEFT]
Dominos is a major past time in Cayo. Teams vie for the championship.

Belikin: The Beer of Belize
[LOWER LEFT]

Customs and immigrations officers welcome visitors at the Western Border
[LOWER RIGHT]

Smash up!
[LOWER RIGHT]
A minor traffic accident may be the biggest news of the day in quiet Cayo.

Iguana
[OPPOSITE UPPER LEFT]
Known locally as bamboo chicken, iguana are plentiful along the rivers of Cayo.

Hawksworth Bridge
[OPPOSITE UPPER RIGHT]
Spanning the magnificent Macal River which separates the towns of Santa Elena and San Ignacio.

Haliconia Flower
[OPPOSITE LOWER LEFT]

Exploring the upper Macal River
[0PPOSITE LOWER RIGHT]

IMMIGRATION - Arrival
MIGRACION - Entrada

San Ignacio Town and Santa Elena
[LEFT]
Located on the banks of the Macal River "Cayo" has all the best of the west.

Peaceful Mennonites
[OPPOSITE UPPER LEFT]
Mennonite farmers eschew life in the fast lane in favor of a slower, more tranquil existence.

San Ignacio Market
[OPPOSITE UPPER RIGHT]
A cornucopia of fresh fruits and vegetables.

Selvin 'Bing' Tzib
[OPPOSITE LOWER LEFT]
Tracing his ancestry to the Yucatec Maya, Bing is well known as one of Cayo's finest tailors.

Rastaman Vibration
[OPPOSITE LOWER RIGHT]
These "Rastas" are respected members of the community but beware the fellows who dress like Rastas but are, in fact, just "rascals" or hustlers.

Belizean-American Friendship Association at Bow Wow Creek
[BELOW]

Photo by Marga

Barton Creek Cave
[LEFT]

Belize is well known among spelunkers and troglophiles as the site of some of the world's largest and most spectacular cave systems. Barton Creek Cave is certainly one of the most beautiful in the country. Most of the exploration is done by canoe as the creek flows through the entire length of the cave. In ancient times the Maya used this cave as a burial site and for the practice of their sacred rituals.

David's Adventure Tours
[BELOW]

Don't worry folks! David's at the wheel!
[OPPOSITE UPPER LEFT]

duPlooy's Jungle Lodge
[OPPOSITE UPPER RIGHT]

Overlooking the Macal river, duPlooy's is typical of the many fine outback lodges making Cayo District a favorite touristic destination.

Clarissa Falls
[OPPOSITE LOWER LEFT AND RIGHT]

Perched on the bank of the Mopan River Clarissa Falls offers fine rustic accomadations and home cooked foods for world travelers.

Transparent-winged Butterfly
[OPPOSITE UPPER LEFT]

Wildflower
[OPPOSITE UPPER RIGHT]

Wildflower
[OPPOSITE LOWER LEFT]

Baby Hummingbird at Nest
[OPPOSITE LOWER RIGHT]

Diurnal Moth
[BELOW]

Calla Creek Road
[RIGHT]
  Winding through pastures and along the Mopan River in the heartland of Cayo District the Cala Creek Road is one of dozens of off the beaten track routes that provide excellent experiences for those who love to walk. Along the way you may stop for a dip in the cool, clean waters of the river, do a bit of birding, and make some new friends among the friendly inhabitants of the area.

Thousand Foot Falls, Mountain Pine Ridge
[OPPOSITE LEFT]

These falls actually plunge over 1600 feet into the Hidden Valley and are the highest in Central America.

Rio On Falls, Mountain Pine Ridge
[OPPOSITE UPPER RIGHT]

The birth place of the Macal and Belize Rivers and an excellent place to take a cool dip on a hot day.

Caracol Maya Ruins
[OPPOSITE LOWER RIGHT]

Surrounded by luxuriant rain forest this is the largest known Maya site in Belize. Caracol covers an area of 88 square miles and had a population of more than 150,000 during the classic period. Some 30,000 structures have been located. This prosperous city-state vied with other centers for regional dominance and won a military victory over Tikal in the year 562 AD. The city was mysteriously abandoned sometime around 950 AD. The largest pyramid, Canaa, rises more than 125 feet in height and is the largest in Belize.

Centipede
[BELOW]

Visiting naturalists new to the forests of Central America should note that while millipedes are quite harmless these centipedes are aggressive predators and are equipped with poison ejecting fangs which can give a nasty sting.

Rio Frio Cave, Mountain Pine Ridge
[RIGHT]

Xunantunich Maya Ruins
[LEFT]

Visiting officers from a British Royal Navy ship survey the remains of the ancient Maya Civilization. Xunantunich means "the Stone Maiden" and was an important Classic Period ceremonial center. Excavations have revealed signs of a major earthquake which occurred here in about 900 AD causing some archaeologists to speculate that this may have been the cause of the cities abandonment. The site is was built upon an artificially flattened hill and includes five plazas.

Xunantunich Maya Ruins
[LOWER LEFT]

El Castillo is the largest structure at Xunantunich and is more than 40 meters high. It remains as one of the largest buildings in Belize.

Hand cranked ferry across the Mopan River
[LOWER RIGHT]

Maya Culture Day at El Pilar
[UPPER LEFT]

El Pilar Maya site is the home of the annual Maya Culture Day. Here a young comedian entertains the crowd.

Annual Festival at San Jose Succotz
[RIGHT]

The "greasy pole" is a popular Belizean tradition and can be seen at many village festivals. A tall pole is covered with lard or grease and a bottle of rum is tied to the top as the prize. Contestants must shinny up the pole all the way to the top. But it turns out that this task is usually extremely difficult and the only way to get up is to organize a crew to stand one upon the other's shoulders in a hilarious feat as the crowd roars with approval.

Annual Festival at San Jose Succotz
[LOWER RIGHT]

We won! Contestants at the annual festival try and capture the "greasy pig." In this particular instance the poor pig, which is supposed to run away from the fellows pursuing it, was not into it and the whole affair turned into a silly fiasco.

Delicious Tamales!
[BELOW]

The regional food of Cayo includes a rich variety of dishes reflecting Mayan, Mexican and Spanish influences.

Calla Creek Foot Bridge
[LEFT]

Stew Chicken with Rice and Beans
[LOWER LEFT]
Jameli Requena serves up the beloved national dish of Belize.

Cayo's Johnny Cash
[LOWER MIDDLE]

Independence Day Marathon Race
[LOWER RIGHT]
Carrying the Belizean Flag participants run the length and breadth of the country in this annual civic event.

Maya Culture Day at El Pilar
[OPPOSITE]
An annual event showcasing traditional dances, foods, and crafts. The "Hog's Head Dance" is always one of the favorites.

Independence Day Event at Belmopan
[UPPER LEFT]
Prime Minister Said Musa reviews the Belize Defense Force Honor Guard.

Swearing In Ceremony, Belmopan.
[LOWER LEFT]
George Price, often referred to as "the father of modern Belize," is sworn in as elder statesman of the Peoples' United Party, PUP, during a special public event installing the new government in 1999.

An Officer of the Belize Defence Force Attends the Independence Day Ceremonies
[LOWER MIDDLE]

Belmopan Government Complex
[LOWER RIGHT]

The Dangriga Turtle Shell Band
[OPPOSITE]
Visiting bands from all four directions entertain at the annual Agricultural Fair at the Belmopan Fairgrounds. The world famous Dangriga Turtle Shell Band plays traditional Garifuna style vibes.

Rasta Rodeo Rider
[UPPER LEFT]
   Cowboys from around the nation compete in the Agricultural Fair Rodeo.

Dog Show
[UPPER RIGHT]
   The competition is intense as highly trained judges determine which show dog will win the the highest honors.

The Annual Agricultural Fair
[LOWER LEFT , RIGHT AND BELOW]

The Blue Hole National Park.
/OPPOSITE UPPER RIGHT AND LEFT]
   A refreshing bathing spot on the Hummingbird Highway. Mopan Maya children frolic in the cool waters.

Hurricane Mitch Floods
[OPPOSITE LOWER LEFT]
   Although Belize was spared most of Mitch's wrath, flooding did occur. Here vehicles attempt to cross Roaring Creek near Belmopan.

From palatial plantation estates and kingly mansions to charming jungle cottages and thatch-roofed Mayan cabins: "Inna Belize, ho is weh dai hat is as roun' di worl'."

Western Highway, Cayo District
[UPPER LEFT]

Bermudian Landing, Belize District
[LOWER LEFT]

Northern Highway, Orange Walk District
[LOWER RIGHT]

Burrell Boom, Belize District
[OPPOSITE]

Western Highway, Belize District
[UPPER LEFT]

Hopkins Village, Stann Creek District
[LOWER LEFT]

San Jose Succotz, Cayo District
[BELOW]

Northern Highway, Belize District
[OPPOSITE UPPER LEFT]

Santa Elena, Cayo District
[OPPOSITE UPPER RIGHT]

Western Highway, Cayo District
[OPPOSITE LOWER LEFT]

San Pedro Columbia, Toledo District
[OPPOSITE LOWER RIGHT]

Garifuna Settlement Day, Dangriga Town
Stann Creek District

The Garifuna people trace their ancestry back to the Western Caribbean where in 1635 two Spanish vessels carrying slaves from Nigeria were shipwrecked off the island of St. Vincent. The survivors took refuge on the island and intermarried with the Amerindian Kalipuna natives thus giving rise to the Garifuna or Garinagu race who look decidedly African but speak an Arawak Indian language. In 1797 British Colonial authorities, tired of fighting with the freedom loving Garifuna, exiled them to Honduras. From there the Garifuna People have colonized nearly the entire coast of Central America. In Belize there are five settlements: Barranco, Sein Bight, Hopkins, Georgetown, and Dangriga. Many Garinagu live in Belize City as well. The Garifuna are the quintessential traveling people. During their entire history they have been on move and this trait continues today as we see strong Garifuna settlements in New York, Chicago, and Los Angeles in the United States. Garifuna Settlement day, on November 19, commemorates their arrival to Belize in 1832 when the great Garinagu hero Alejo Benji led his people out of Honduras to the new promise land of British Honduras. Settlement day is now one of the most important celebrations in Belize and this is especially true at Dangriga where the event is really massive with parades, music, traditional foods, dances and all night drumming sessions.

Garifuna Settlement Day

Several parades and many important cultural events mark this as the most important of the years celebrations among the Garifuna People. At dawn canoes festooned with palm branches and decorations appear from the horizon and make their way to the shore as drummers aboard keep up the solemn beat. When they reach the beach they are greeted by a large crowd and then every one marches gayly through the streets on their way to the church where a special Mass is held. As part of the church event a harvest festival is enacted giving thanks to God for the years abundant food. In 1999 the Settlement Day Mass in Dangriga was conducted by His Lordship, Bishop O.P. Martin and his concelebrants.

Our Father: *Waguchi le siélubei, inebewala biri, chülüha barueihan woun. Adügüwala le babusuenrun kaisi ladügüniwa sielu. Ruboun waigan fein woun ugune to lanina sagü weyu. Ferudunbei wachara kaisi ferundun wamaniña woun. Madundehabawa lidoun lémeri figou, pero safabawa sun würibani.*

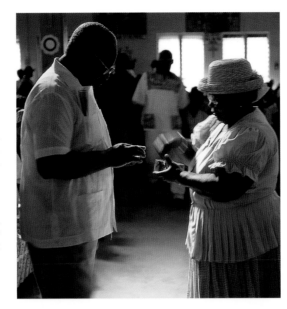

Woman's Dance Troupe
Garifuna Settlement Day
Dangriga Town, Stann Creek District
[LEFT]

Mary Ann Lambe, Miss Garifuna 1998-99
[OPPOSITE LEFT]
   In order to win the crown of Miss Garifuna contestants must show proficiency in a variety of cultural traditions including sacred dance, oratory skill, and skits depicting important Garifuna myths and legends.

Miss Sacred Heart, Dangriga, 1998-99
[OPPOSITE UPPER MIDDLE]

Miss Dangriga, 1998-99
[OPPOSITE UPPER RIGHT]

Dreadlock Style, Dangriga
[OPPOSITE LOWER RIGHT]

Fishing Boats at Stann Creek
[UPPER LEFT]

Dangriga Town
[LOWER LEFT AND RIGHT]

"L. K." The Lyrical King, Stann Creek District Day
[OPPOSITE UPPER MIDDLE]
   Hailing from Sein Bight, L.K. is the Garifuna master of Roots and Culture and his Rastaman Rapping keeps the crowd's feet tapping and fingers snapping at the District Day Dance at the Dangriga Beach Bashing! Strictly Roots and Culture, Yaa!

Thrill Rides at the Annual Dangriga Festival
[OPPOSITE UPPER RIGHT]

Garifuna Women from Barranco Village Perform Traditional Dances Stann Creek District Day
[OPPOSITE LOWER LEFT]

Greasy Pole, Dangriga Style
[OPPOSITE LOWER RIGHT]
The "greasy pole" is a competitive event and common feature during village festivals around the country. Here, in this Dangriga version, the pole is horizontal not vertical and extends over the water. As always, a bottle of rum hangs at the end as the prize to whoever is able to reach it without falling into the waves.

Ereba!
[LEFT AND UPPER MIDDLE]

The beloved ereba cassava bread which is the traditional staple food of the Garifuna. Here its preparation and cooking are being demonstrated at the annual Culture Day.

Tortillas Calientes!
[LOWER MIDDLE]

Mopan-Maya woman prepares delicious hot tortillas of freshly milled corn.

Forest Fire Observation Tower
Near Big Creek
[BELOW]

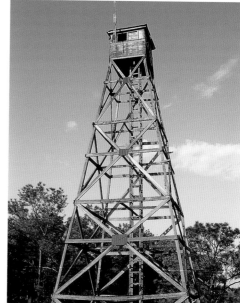

The Southern Highway
[UPPER RIGHT]

The Southern Highway runs south from Dangriga and is the gateway to the Belizean Outback and the remote (until recently) Toledo District. Here the jungle still reins supreme and Maya village life continues much as it has for thousands of years

Cockscomb Basin Wildlife Sanctuary
[LOWER RIGHT]

Young naturalist, Delmiro Nunez from Hopkins Village, explores the pristine swamp habitat which provides refuge to one of the countries largest populations of jaguar.

Fresh Plantain Chips
[BELOW]

Pine-ridge Savannah Along the Manatee Road
[OPPOSITE UPPER LEFT]

James Bus Line Providing Transport South
[OPPOSITE UPPER RIGHT]

Golden Stream Mopan Maya Village
[OPPOSITE LOWER LEFT AND RIGHT]

Marie Sharp's Famous
Belizean Habanero Sauce
[UPPER RIGHT]

Produced in the fertile paradise of the Stann Creek Valley Marie Sharp's red habanero is considered to be the hottest variety of pepper known to man. Marie has spent many years cultivating an habanero worthy of her unique carrot based recipe which achieves the perfect balance betweenheat and flavor.

Banana Flower
[LOWER LEFT]

Processing Stann Creek Valley Oranges
[LOWER MIDDLE AND RIGHT]

Boom Creek
[OPPOSITE UPPER LEFT]

Victoria Peak Seen from the Coastal Brackish
Marsh Near Hopkins Village
[OPPOSITE UPPER RIGHT]

Hopkins Village, The Heartland of
Garinagu Culture
[OPPOSITE LOWER LEFT AND RIGHT]

Independence Day Parade, Hopkins Village
[UPPER RIGHT]

Young Mr. Francisco Nunez of Hopkins with
Miss Trisha of Tippletree Beya
[LOWER MIDDLE]

Little Creole Boy from Gales Point Manatee
[LOWER RIGHT]

Kek' chi Maya Girl From Blue Creek Village
[LOWER LEFT]

Butterfly On Haliconia
[OPPOSITE LEFT]

Hummingbird
[OPPOSITE UPPER RIGHT]

Cockscomb Basin Wildlife Sanctuary
[OPPOSITE LOWER RIGHT]
A hiker surveys the eerie crash site of an ill-fated flight that met disaster.

Fallen Stones Butterfly Farm
[UPPER RIGHT]
Located near the ruins of Lubaantun, Fallen Stones Butterfly Ranch produces a variety of butterflies which are exported live, in the chrysalis stage, to Europe. Manager Juan Coy gives a tour of the facility.

Belize Aquaculture, LTD.
[BELOW AND LOWER RIGHT]
Located across the lagoon from the Placencia Peninsula at Blare Atholl, Belize Aquaculture is a new cutting edge "green" industry producing some of the worlds highest yields of export quality shrimp while at the same time protecting the local ecology. A scientifically designed system uses innovative techniques to prevent effects harmful to the local habitat. Belize Aquaculture is a model industry which proves that it is possible to have economic development, provide jobs and earn much needed foreign exchange without causing a negative impact on the environment.

Toledo District Day
[LEFT]

A young member of the Ebolite Dance Troupe performs with grace and style at Punta Gorda.

Garifuna drumming
[BELOW]

The main Garifuna music form is the intricate Afro-Caribbean drumming which always accompanies a special event. Drum sessions may go on all night long as the hypnotic beat summons up the spiritual world and dancers are inspired to reveal the unseen forces.

Wanaragu Dance
[OPPOSITE]

Known as the Wanaragu Dance in the Garifuna community and the John Canoe Dance among the Creoles, this tradition seems to be of African origin and is primarily seen around Christmas and New Years. The dance is still practiced in several of the islands of the Caribbean such as Jamaica. It is set to a lively rhythm and restricted to a few formal steps and depends for effect on exaggerated body movements..

Punta Gorda Town
[OPPOSITE UPPER LEFT]
   A Kek'Chi Maya Indian family comes to town for market day where they sell their agricultural products and purchase supplies unavailable in their village.

Placencia Town
[OPPOSITE UPPER RIGHT]

Punta Gorda Market
[OPPOSITE LOWER LEFT]

Punta Gorda Town
[OPPOSITE LOWER RIGHT]

Garifuna Fishermen ply Amatique Bay in search of a good catch
[UPPER RIGHT]

Fishing by the pier at Punta Gorda Town
[LOWER RIGHT]

Morpho Butterfly Wing (detail)
[BELOW]

Maya Indian Children Fish and Play by the Rio Grande Near San Miguel Village
[OPPOSITE]

Heading inland from Punta Gorda toward the Maya Mountains we enter the magical world of the Mopan and Kek'chi Indians. Luxuriant vegetation and pristine, crystal clear rivers provide an environment where life, in all its forms, flourishes. In the villages many ancient Mayan customs are preserved in life-style, food, housing, and language.

Kek'chi Maya Dance Masks
[BELOW]

The kek'Chi Maya Indians of Toledo District trace their roots back to the Province of Alta Verapaz in Guatemala. Every Maya Village has its annual festival in honor of the Patron Saint. During these festivals a variety of masked dances are performed such as the Dance of the Conquest, the Deer Dance and the Dance of the Moors. These sacred dances recount stories about the Mayan supernatural pantheon, the history of the Mayan People, and important myths which form the foundation of their identity.

The Rio Grande Near San Miguel Village, Toledo District
[RIGHT]

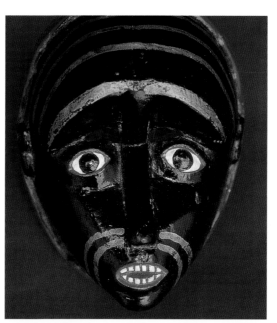

Kek' chi Indian Ceremonial Masks
[LEFT AND UPPER MIDDLE]

Nim Li Punit Maya Ruins
[LOWER MIDDLE]

The ruins of Nim Li Punit were not discovered until 1976 and since then many artifacts and several tombs have been unearthed. Located on a high ridge, the site commands a beautiful view of the coastal plain to the southeast. The Maya caretaker leads visitors in the exploration of a recently discovered tomb.

Nim Li Punit Maya Ruins
[BELOW]

Detail of Late Classic period stela 15. This sandstone monolith, which was erected in 721 AD, contains a carving of an imposing figure performing a sacred ritual by dropping an offering of corn kernels or copal incense into an elaborately adorned censer which rests on the back of a grotesque underworld monster. "Nim Li Punit" means "Big Hat" in the Kek'chi-Maya language and refers to the headgear worn by the priests depicted on the stela.

Blue Creek Rainforest Field Station
[RIGHT]

Cecilio Coc, a native Mayan naturalist who works at the Interntional Zoological Expedition's field Station near Punta Gorda, leads a team of biologists along a system of suspension bridges nearly 100 feet above Blue Creek and the forest floor for a unique tour of the rain forest canopy.

The Crystal Skull of Lubaantun
[MIDDLE]

Santiago, the Mayan caretaker of the ruins of Lubaantun, displays his photograph of the enigmantic crystal skull supposedly discovered at the site by the daughter of F. A. Mitchell-Hedges in the year 1926 as her father led a British Museum Expedition. Although most archaeologists dismiss the skull as a fake there continues to be considerable controversy concerning the artifact. The skull was subjected to the scrutiny of a team of scientists some years ago and their findings were astonishing. It seems that whoever made the skull carved it against the natural grain in a process that is virtually impossible even by the most modern methods. The mystery continues...

Lubaantun Maya Ruins
[BELOW]

Lubaantun means "fallen stones" in the Mayan language. It is located on a high ridge and from the top of the highest temple you can see the Caribbean Ocean more than 20 miles distant. The site includes five main plazas and three ball courts. The architecture at Lubaantun is unusual in several aspects: the stones were laid without the use of mortar requiring great precision and the corners of many of the temples feature soft, rounded edges. It is thought that Lubaantun was only briefly occupied from 700 to 890 AD at the end of the Classic Period.

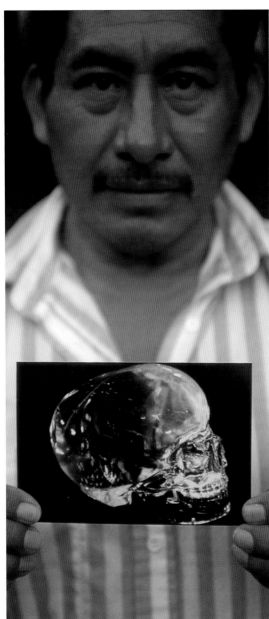

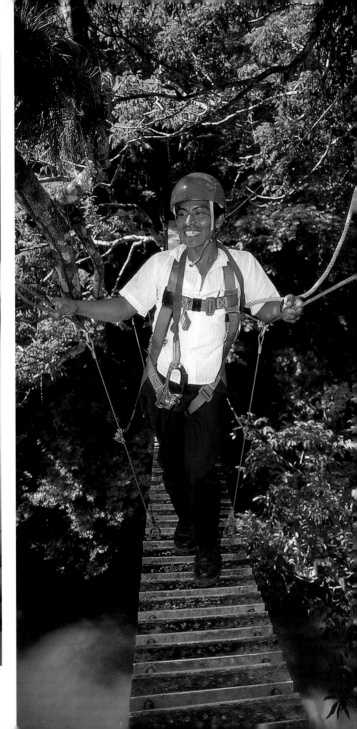

Like a string of shimmering pearls dozens of palm fringed islands line the largest barrier reef in the Americas

The great barrier reef of Belize is one of the largest and most important marine ecosystems on Earth. Declared a World Heritage Site by UNESCO in 1996, the reef's aquatic habitat is a paradise for divers, fishermen, sailors, and beachcombers. The largest inhabited islands are Ambergris Caye and Caye Caulker where tourism has become an important industry. Many other exclusive resorts, research stations, and fishing camps have been established on smaller cayes up and down the coast. The reef runs the entire length of the Belize coastline at a distance of 10 to 25 miles from the mainland. Several protected areas have been declared including Bacalar Chico National Park and Hol Chan Marine Park. East of the barrier reef lie two atolls: Turneffe Islands and Lighthouse Reef, home of the Half Moon Caye Natural Monument.

English Caye
[LEFT]

Goffs Caye
[OPPOSITE UPPER LEFT]

Saint Georges Caye
[OPPOSITE UPPER RIGHT]
Site of the decisive battle in which the Spanish Fleet was repeled and the future existence of the British Colony was insured. *Shoulder to Shoulder* was the battle cry as the colony's inhabitants fought valiantly against the aggressor and finally through bravery, wit, and the grace of God, were to prevail.

Colson Cays
[OPPOSITE LOWER LEFT]

Caye Caulker
[OPPOSITE LOWER RIGHT]

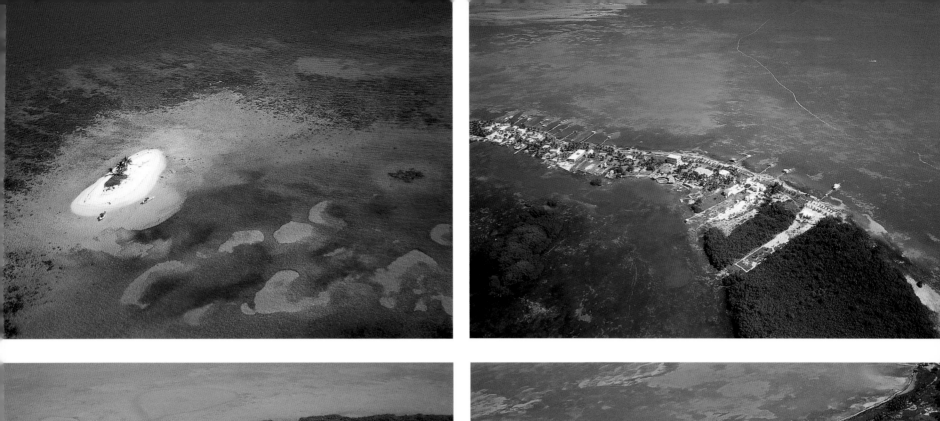

San Pedro, Ambergris Caye

San Pedro has for many years now been the premier touristic destination in Belize. Located near the southern end of Ambergris Caye, San Pedro was once upon a time a small, quiet fishing village. Then, in the early seventies, it was "discovered" by divers and fishermen drawn by the pristine beauty of the island and the barrier reef. Within a few years a booming tourist industry emerged.

The town itself is located on the eastern side of the island facing the reef which is located just off shore. The reef provides excellent protection for marine craft and this has made San Pedro a favorite destination for visiting yachts. The main street is lined by quaint shops. The town park is presided over by the Patron Saint. Dozens of first class hotels and superb restaurants abound. Just South of town is a little magic land called San Telmo founded by legendary *San Pedrano* Musician Señor Severino.

Caye Caulker

Located just south of Ambergris Caye, Cauker is another little fishing village that has undergone major changes during the last several decades due to tourism development. Caye Caulker still maintains the atmosphere of a small fishing village and is a favorite destination for young tourists who prefer a more "laid back" destination. Lobster and conch fishing became big business during the seventies and this along with the tourist trade have brought prosperity to the island. Manatee and rainbow parrot fish are common in this area. Sun drenched days and magnificent sunsets make Caye Caulker a tropical island dreamland.

My first visit to Belize was during a solo motorcycle tour of the Americas in the year of 1973. After a few months traveling through the "Latin American" land of Mexico it was a surprise to arrive at the boarder of British Honduras and be greeted by polite, English speaking officials. The Colony in 1973 was quite a bit different than the Belize we know today. Quiet, peaceful, supporting a tiny population, British Honduras was a land yet to be discovered by the outside world and a well kept secret by the few travelers, like myself, who came to know and love her for all her unique beauty, charm and quirkiness. I remember enjoying the abundant seafood and the traditional rice and beans cooked with coconut milk. I remember being captivated by the, for me, exotic Creole, Mestizo, Garifuna, Maya, British, and East Indian cultures I encountered during my explorations. I found the Belizean people to be remarkably friendly and courteous, well educated, and always hospitable and helpful. In 1973 agriculture was in its infancy and a lot of packaged and canned foods were imported from Britain. Tourism was just getting started in British Honduras and was pretty much limited to San Pedro which had become famous as a base for scuba divers and sport fishermen exploring the pristine reef. The interior was virgin territory for a young traveler. I had a particular interest in tropical nature and the rain forests of Belize I found full of strange and marvelous places and creatures. The whole mix, something ineffable and charming about Belize, captured my imagination and I found myself returning over and over again during the following years.

Visiting with Anselma, Francisco and Anita Nunez at Hopkins Village

Photo: Tricia of Tippletree

In 1981 I sailed down from New York City in my small trimaran sailboat and for the next ten years spent several months a year cruising along the reef and exploring the waterways. I remember many sublime sunsets anchored off an uninhabited caye. I remember watching frolicking manatee in the lagoon adjacent to Gales Point. And I remember more than once having a great time accompanying British soldiers during their notorious "pub crawls" in San Pedro and Placencia!

In 1983 I established an ecology and conservation organization with a local operation called the Belize Wildlife Defense Project. Over the years we have produced and distributed free in Belize tens of thousands of conservation posters, such as the nationwide "Belize is My Home Too" campaign and presently we are developing an ambitious environmental education program for Central America designed to promote green awareness.

FAST FORWARD to the year 2000. Much has changed in Belize. She has now become (since 1981) an independent nation and is going through all the stages of exploring her newly won freedom: experiencing all the challenges, trials, and joys of infancy and youth. Agricultural development now provides an abundance of fresh produce. The seafood export industry, especially of lobster, shrimp, and conch, has brought rapid prosperity to the coastal and island settlements. Tourism is booming, as Belize is now one of the world's top ten adventure travel destinations. Ecology has become the National passion and the Belizean environment remains clean and pure. All the elements necessary for a peaceful and prosperous future are abundantly present in Belize and the rich cultural and natural heritage that God has given her will prove that the saying "strength through diversity" is true.

The photographs in this book were taken over many years and many Belizeans have provided help and encouragement. I wish to thank all my friends in Belize for making me feel at home and making my explorations possible.

I wish to express special thanks to pioneer Belizean entrepreneur and ecologist Mr. Barry Bowen for agreeing to finance the publication of this book. Mr. Bowen has distinguished himself for investing in "green" industries such as the ecologically minded Rain Forest Coffee Project at his Gallon Jug Experimental Farm and for the innovative and environmentally sensitive Belize Aquaculture Project at Blare Atholl which produces record breaking high yields of the world's finest shrimp while at the same time protecting the local habitat.